Sales Funnel Strategies

How To Easily Apply Sales Funnels To Your Business

Mark F. Zimmerman

What Is A Sales Funnel?

We make use of the metaphor of a sales funnel (wide at the very top, narrow at the end) to monitor the sales process.

Towards the top of this funnel you've got 'unqualified prospects' - the people who you believe may need your service or product, but to whom you've never spoken. At the end of this funnel, many delivery and sales steps after, you've got those who've received the service or product and have also purchased it.

The metaphor of a funnel can be utilized because prospects drop out of different stages of an extended sales process.

Using the sales funnel, and by calculating the amount of leads at every point of the procedure, you are able to predict the amount of prospects who'll, over time, become clients.

A lot more than this, by taking a look at how these amounts change with time, you are able to spot issues in the sales pipeline and just take corrective action early.

For instance, in the event that you spot that not many mailings were actioned during a month, you may be expecting that, in a couple of months time, sales may dry out. The following month, you can ensure that more mailings than usual are sent.

Utilization of the Sales Funnel shows obstacles and dead time, or if they're an insufficient quantity of leads at any point. This knowledge enables you to decide where sales agents should focus their attention and efforts to help keep sales at the required level and, also, to satisfy targets.

The funnel may also explain where improvements have to be implemented in the sales procedure. These might be as straightforward as introducing extra sales coaching or making certain sales reps put adequate emphasis on each step of the process.

The very first stage in establishing sales funnel reporting would be to brainstorm the sales process together with your sales and marketing people to make certain that it is correct and comprehensive.

Out of this, find out the main sequential parts of the sales procedure and, from these, generate status codes. Then, label your leads using these codes (this is easier when you've got a sales contact management system). Finally, work-out the amount of prospects of every status and calculate the change from the last month.

As you develop an image of a sales funnel from every month, you can begin to comprehend where you are able to enhance your sales process. Obviously, a product is required before you can start to sell anything though, and this is what we are going to discuss in the following chapters.

What is Internet Commerce

The idea of internet commerce is about going online to complete business better and faster. It is all about giving clients controlled use of your pc systems and allowing them to serve themselves. It's about making your organization commit to a significant on-line effort and integrating your website with the essence of your business. Should you do this, you will notice results!

The web is a feasible alternative to all of the conventional ways of conducting business. Can't meet in person? Send an e-mail with a photograph attached. When it's time for the customer to purchase the merchandise, make use of a secured server for charge card and, sometimes even, digital cash payments! The opportunities and situations through which internet business can be done are limitless.

In the wonderful world of internet commerce, the area where you conduct business are Websites. Most businesses exist already offline. Adding an internet site represents a way to improve their business. For Online start-ups, the website may be the only place they conduct business.

To do business, additionally, you need a method to accept orders and action payment. In a store, clients simply discover the products and services they need, enter a queue at the till and pay the shop clerk. In internet commerce, orders need to be placed and items shipped. Orders are often handled through interactive, internet-based forms.

Clients in a store pay by cash, check or credit / debit cards. Online clients can't pay by check or cash, only through electronic means. Internet commerce transactions have to occur through secure electronic connections and special merchant portals for processing payment.

Delivery fulfilment, in the wonderful world of internet commerce, is harder than in conventional stores, requiring shipping and transportation much like catalogue and mail order companies.

In both regular commerce and internet commerce, you need to locate a method to attract clients to you. This is epitomized by your online marketing strategy.

On the internet, one simple way to do this is via Google Adwords, where you research keywords related to your site that attract significant numbers of monthly searches. Google will then rank your site higher in their listings when a user enters that keyword into a search and you pay Google a certain amount for every click you receive.

You can also market your site by writing articles related to it and posting these (with a link back to your site in your bio) on well-known article directory sites like EzineArticles.com. These sites are free and usually rank well in the search engines.

What Can I Sell

Everyone who sets up an internet business has to address the question: What should I sell? And just about everyone appears to incur 2 classic errors at first:

They sell what everybody else is trying to sell: electronics, designer clothing and DVD's. What they find is a marketplace already saturated with these products and the suppliers usually don't work in small quantities. To create any profit at all, they'd need to buy huge quantities.

They sell what they know and love. Regrettably, unless there's a significant demand for what they know and love, they will be stuck with lots of product they are able to appreciate but can not move.

The following 'hotspots' could keep you connected with what individuals are buying, what things are up-and-coming and what things are declining in popularity. If your opinions all originate from a couple of places, you are limiting your-self so expand your thinking. You may consider taking a look at one of these simple hotspots for inspiration:

Newspapers. You will get a concept of what's on the minds of consumers simply by reading the life-style section, the business pages or taking a look at the adverts the big stores are putting out.

Consumer Publications. You will find countless magazines based around specialised products and services, specific hobbies and special interest markets. They have been a good resource for building niche products.

Shopping Arcades / Bricks-and-mortar stores. Communicate with the salespeople, discover what is being sold. You may also source your suppliers off the boxes. Obtain the wholesaler's name, ring them and get the name of their local distributor in your town.

Trend-spotting sites, such as Influxinsights.com, Trendhunter.com and Trendwatching.com.

The entertainment industry, films and television fuel product trends. Knowing what's being released in the movie industry, you can begin sourcing related products and services prior to the trend beginning.

Imdb.com maintains a list of movies that are going to be released in the coming year. So, if you are aware now that particular movies are going to be released, you can begin stocking up on related products prior to them becoming expensive, like Superman, Batman, Star Wars and Curious George.

It's wise to own a notebook for product sourcing, be it a hand-held note book or a PDA, to record your thoughts when they come to you. Ninety percent of the ideas you don't jot down can get lost. When you are visiting these hot-spots for ideas, if you notice hundreds of ideas for products to market, you will not have the ability to recall all of those. You need to write them down in your product sourcing notebook, then return to them and begin researching.

Clickbank

ClickBank is utilized by over 10, 000 web companies and 100, 000 affiliates to provide their services and products immediately on the internet, with Ebooks and computer software the primary purchases.

Anybody can join ClickBank being an affiliate - it's free. Whenever you look for a product that you intend to promote, either at a vendor's web site or by searching through the ClickBank Marketplace, you'll be given a particular link that you simply use to send clients to the merchandise page.

The very first thing you must do is to register for a ClickBank account. This is to ensure that ClickBank can send you payments. Payment is sent every 14 days.

Now you will be ready to promote ClickBank products and services and earn commission. The market listings are displayed by popularity, to help you easily note which would be the items most in-demand.

Against each entry is a link to create a hoplink which gives you the amount of commission you'll obtain upon selling that item and your affiliate link.

You need to target products and services with an acceptable rate of commission, no less than 25%, to ensure your time and efforts are worthwhile.

Affiliates can easily add the ClickBank services or products to their sites or their adverts and earn commission (as much as 75%) on the sales. They are able to also earn money as a reseller by referring other affiliates and vendors to ClickBank.

Vendors may utilize Clickbank to take care of the complete ordering procedure and to manage their affiliate schemes. Clickbank will pay sales commission, automatically, to every affiliate who connects a paying client to the seller. Clickbank charges the client, pays the vendor, and pays the affiliate.

Among the explanations why Clickbank is loved is due to its' robust marketplace (a large number of affiliates can easily see and promote your product). To be a merchant, you'd be having to pay a one-time fee of $49.

95. Probably, that's all you'll ever pay.

The draw-back, however, is that Clickbank will take a commission from every one of your sales, which will be around 10% (at this time). Also, tempting affiliates is quite difficult with a minimum of a 50% commission required to even have them interested.

Clickbank is one of the many digital product sites on the web. Other similar websites include: CupidPlc.com, Addynamo.com, Cj.com, Shareasale.com, Linkshare.com, Associateprograms.com, Affiliatescout.com, Paydotcom.com, Tradedoubler.com and Affiliatewindow.com.

To sum up, Clickbank is a good network, with an easy and simple to access system, easy registration process and good support. While there are some things that can be improved, over all Clickbank is a really usable network ideal for people first starting out in internet marketing.

Drop Shipping

Today, drop shipping is really as popular as it ever was. The primary ingredients for an effective drop-shipping business are: a great, reliable drop-shipping company, a sales funnel (mainly e-bay) and, the most crucial ingredient, the client.

Without drop-shipping, you are able to be an e-bay member and create a good income on-line, but with a drop-shipping company, you have even more products available. Having a great drop-shipper is excellent, since there is no inventory needed by you because all sales and delivery are looked after by the drop-shipper.

Do not alter the tech specs of any products supplied by the drop shipping company, but be sure you put an alternative description to the merchandise in order to give it a distinctive feel from what other sellers are utilizing.

Any photo's of products you have already been provided with for sale, should also be produced to appear dissimilar to the rest of the sellers on e-bay who might be utilizing the same drop-shipper as you. This could probably incorporate an ad-rotator.

Make certain, before you begin to market any items on e-bay, that you always check the costs of the other sellers on-line, as well as the buying price of the retailers where you live.

Whenever you now get sales for the products,

all you have to do would be to pay the drop-shipper his or her price for the merchandise and keep the difference between your drop-shipper's price and that which you charged the client as your profit.

Once you have become proficient with trying to sell drop-shipping items on e-bay, you'll then have the ability to start and sell things on a bigger scale. This really is ok, however, you must keep in mind that you'll have to pay e-bay for the privilege of allowing you to sell and display your products and services on the site.

You need to ensure that deliveries from the drop shipper are on time and that the products reach your clients in an acceptable state, otherwise the reputation you have on-line might suffer, making sales in the future difficult.

There are several guides available on Clickbank about Drop Shipping that are worth checking out. These include: 'The Drop Ship Guide', which takes you through the basics of setting up your own drop shipping business step-by-step; and 'Drop Shipping 4 Idiots', which is a comprehensive course covering all aspects of the industry, including insider product sourcing secrets and dozens of high traffic places where you can list and sell your products for free.

Being a truly successful seller is what you are targeting so, with a great drop-shipper and e-bay working together, you have everything you require to flourish because this is a winning combination for a sales-force.

Affiliate Marketing

You may have heard that affiliate marketing is among the easiest ways to generate an income on the internet. Listed here are the steps to carrying it out your-self:

Select a specialized niche

By this, we mean a particular group of individuals that you're targeting. This group will have an interest in a specific product or information that one can sell to them. Types of these items include: cameras, Kindle, ebooks about love, editing computer software and so on.

In selecting a niche, you have to be as specific as you are able to be. You shouldn't be too broad since the competition will, undoubtedly, be very fierce. Be very particular and become a big fish in a small pond.

Put up your site or weblog

Before you do any-thing, you'll first want a weblog or, even better, an internet site. Do not worry if you know nothing about web development, because creating a web-site isn't (any longer) as hard as you believe it is. A total newbie is now able to easily create a web-site. You must have an internet site so you can have an online shop where you are able to sell your affiliate products and services.

All you need to do here is obtain a domain name. In selecting a domain name, it is best to work with a phrase that relates to your niche.

In online marketing, this is known as key words. You are able to research rich key words on Google Adwords.

Rich key words describe phrases which have a large amount of monthly searches but just a few sites using them. These should be your target. When you found have a great one, you are able to go and obtain that domain from any domain store like Go-Daddy.

After having a domain name, you have to host your website somewhere (we suggest you try Hostgator). After that, you can use Wordpress to style your website.

Join affiliate marketing websites

After establishing your website, you are able to join affiliate marketing websites like ClickBank, Amazon, Commission Junction,

Linkshare, and so on. Just search for the products, be they physical or digital, that you desire to sell. Get those products and place them on your website.

Sell affiliate products on your site

The great thing about internet marketing is that you are able to just grab products from affiliate sites, free of charge, then sell them on your websites. Just make your reviews, tutorials, (or whatever) on your site to advertise those products. Then, once a visitor comes and buys the products you are promoting, you'll make some commission.

So that's how simple affiliate marketing is. The thing you need here, however, is effort and patience. It won't cause you to get rich quickly but, if you really put some effort into it, you will profit over the long run.

The Link Between Products, Key Words and Prospects

Finding success in e-commerce can be boiled right down to one theme: Identify the prospect's requirements and supply an answer for them. It is that easy. You need to print that statement out and fix it across your monitor. In the event that you stray out of this theme, you'll have issues earning money.

Key-word research may be the key to pinpointing the prospect's requirements. When doing the keyword study, you need to identify the phrases they're using to find answers to their needs. Most people appreciate this concept, but neglect to advance the procedure.

Lots of folks have said they don't wish to pursue rankings under some key words because they don't feature such products or services. Should you have ever said this as well, you are ruining things for yourself.

Remember, we're pinpointing the requirements of prospects. If we don't have services or products oriented to an easily identified need then we determine, through key word research, what we should do! We must get these products and services, or decide on a method to acquire the service!

Assume we now have a website trying to sell hiking and backpacking gear. We now have backpacks, guide books, tents etc. When conducting our key word research, we discover our prospects will also be searching for hiking journals by which they are able to describe their hikes. As we do not stock hiking journals, you want to omit those key words, correct? NO!

You want to look for a type of writing journal for hiking and add them to the catalogue of products and services. Rather than looking upon this keyword discovery as an irrelevance, you should see it as a chance to expand your product line and create a new revenue stream.

We value our prospects, which means providing them with answers to all their needs. In so doing, they'll return to our site over and over once they require more hiking gear.

One of the hardest concepts for web-masters to understand is the truth that you shouldn't design your website predicated on your opinion of your industry. Your prospects should design it. By this, I am talking about the value of using key-word research to determine all of the products and / or services you will offer.

Often, a bit of simple keyword research can throw up some unique angles relating to your business that you would never have thought of yourself. Recognize and utilize this to your advantage to better fulfil market demand.

Discover what your prospects are looking for and ignore anything else. Follow this advice and your website will transform into a cash machine.

The Front and Back of Sales Funnels

The sales funnel is really a methodical marketing procedure where you systematically qualify your prospects in to clients and, additionally, refine them in to hyper-responsive clients. Your client base gets smaller as your bottom line increases as you provide more expensive products to your hyper-responsive clients.

The front-end may be the most dynamic facet of your sales funnel and the part that needs continuous experimentation. You will find, literally, endless front-end methods, restricted purely by your imagination and resources.

The focus at your front end would be to attract and qualify people who possess an inclination to buy your items further down the sales funnel.

Generally, the qualification happens whenever a person opts-in to get something from you. It's this opt in stage that turns your every day web surfer right into a lead, given that they've just carried out an action indicating that they, at the very least, possess some desire to have what you've got.

There are all types of front end marketing tools: becoming a member of a contact newsletter, subscribing to a weblog via RSS or email notifications, opting-in together with your name and email to down-load a complimentary report, registering for a totally free on-line service or ticking a box to get more information in regards to a product / topic when subscribing to something (co-registration).

The front end involves attracting attention and enticing people in to the sales funnel. But, generally, it's in the back end where, in fact, the profits are created.

Your back end consists of your more expensive items. Essentially, we're referring to meeting exactly the same demand (inside a niche), just with alternative media. This may include information distributed via audio, visually, live or privately.

The particular distinction between your front end and the back end is about the kind of customer and the cost paid.

In the back end, all of your clients have

travelled through the front end, tried your complimentary materials, bought a basic level service or product and also have experienced substantial value from what you've offered. So much so, that they're wanting to purchase again from you.

It's common that only a tiny percent, say 1-2%, of the entire people entering your front end will end up in the back end. That's ok, because that small group are spending a lot of money. While front end products and services may cost under $100, back end products are often priced in the hundreds or thousands.

The back end is the main profit source for business since it is stable and predictable and this is the major reason for establishing a back end to begin with.

Sales Funnel Success

Sales funnels are, basically, just a blueprint for your lead to sale procedure. You can start with, say, one thousand leads (i.e. site visitors). One hundred of these leads may click on the sales page url for your product, fifty could click on the 'Order Now' button and be taken to the shopping cart and 10 might actually finish the sales process and purchase the product. If your funnel begins with 1000 prospects and finishes with 10 sales, then that is a 1% conversion ratio.

In reality, though, the sales funnels for most online businesses are actually very complex.

This due to all the different kinds of website traffic that visit websites, the various kinds of behaviour that need to be assessed, the buy and connection outcomes and the number of varied ways a visitor may become a buyer.

To produce a more streamlined sales funnel, you firstly have to identify each and every way people can enter the funnel, see where they've originated from, what their agenda is and where they're at in the purchase cycle.

Then, you need to identify every activity that somebody can undertake on the website: read some content, read more content, contribute to a newsletter, view a social networking profile, buy something, or exit the website.

Finally, you ought to identify the measures to place on every activity: the time on the page, the entry path, the exit path, etc.

Then, you analyse this info and come up with all of the different pathways a visitor may take during your funnel. The key is to not change your website yet.

When a funnel is designed and the systems have been put in place, start compiling reports at each stage to comprehend how your funnel operates in reality.

Try out this in your weblog. Once you've collated enough information to begin making decisions, I guarantee you will see obvious points of failure in your process and they're likely to appear in two main areas:

1) A webpage that does an excellent job at encouraging a different behaviour (i.e. instead of keeping somebody in the sales funnel).

2) A webpage that, basically, does not move a person to another part of the funnel.

Initially, you'll probably feel as if there's a lot to get through, so you'll have to prioritize the changes you wish to make. Concentrate on the areas which are costing you the largest quantity of sales (which might be at the end of the funnel).

With effort, focus and time you can see huge improvements in the performance of your site and never have to attract one new visitor. Sounds good doesn't it?

Sales Funnel Planning

A sales funnel can only flourish in an industry where there's a demand for the product you offer. If you're yet to locate your market niche, you should concentrate on choosing one.

When you are happy you've got a profitable niche, you can start work on crafting your sales funnel.

Your primary focus is definitely meeting the requirements of the customer. Across the funnel, you do that with more and more specifically tailored products and services. Your capability to charge high ticket prices and maximize profit rests on developing quality back-end products and services.

Initially, a need may appear quite broad, however, when you dig deeper you may find that it's actually an extremely specific facet of the overall problem that many people face. Having an in-depth knowledge of the most popular issues your visitors face when trying to meet an over-all need, allows you to know what products and services to offer.

After you have a summary of the most typical issues in your market, you could start to plan how better to deal with them. Think about delivering solutions utilizing varied media, like: downloadable video or audio, text, telephone or face-to-face conferences, private tuition or workshops.

A typical practice in the front end of a sales funnel for an internet business, is to pay attention to digital goods. You create the merchandise once and, assuming it remains current, it's set-and-forget.

As you move down the funnel, you are able to still utilize digital items to fulfil your super-responsive clients, but maybe with more bespoke content (a much more specialised problem), or by providing your innovative methods or supplying a bigger package of content all together.

Broadly speaking, as clients move towards the back-end, particularly if you operate an information publishing business predicated on your expertise, they'll be prepared to receive more personalized attention. The back-end is usually where private coaching or small workshops work nicely. You are able to gather an extremely small number of your general customer base, who are ready to pay well and work with you in a far more personalised format.

To begin building your sales funnel, you'll need to look beyond that first sale and see the picture as a whole. The procedure is flexible and takes effort and testing. A great sales funnel will tap all of the correct triggers (empathy, social proof) in the folks who have the requirement for your product. With that degree of clarity, you'll be able to produce a perception that you provide the best answer for them and can charge a high ticket price.

Putting Your Theory to Practice

As you will have gathered by now, the sales funnel is the key to success on the internet. We know the theory that it is a stage-by-stage procedure for attracting the attention of prospects and converting them into clients. So, in this chapter, we will look at the actual steps required for its' practical implementation.

Marketing

You need to use marketing strategies such as: PPC Adverts (Google, Twitter, Facebook, Youtube), Banners, Blogging and Forum

Posts. Draw in your traffic using those tactics and send it all to your individual capture page.

Your individual capture page

Your Sales Funnel should be set-up to capture the prospect's information. A capture page has an opt-in form for the prospect to input their private information. These details get automatically used in your email Auto-responder. When somebody entered your sales funnel to be a prospect, they literally decided to receive some kind of communication from you. This is permission marketing whenever your prospects provide you with the permission to make contact with them with further materials.

Your Email Auto-responder

You will find various kinds of auto-responders. Typically, the most popular are AWeber and Getresponse. I take advantage of AWeber. It's among the most significant marketing tools. Utilizing an auto-responder enables you to construct a list of potential buyers and begin creating a relationship together.

Follow-up and Develop a Relationship

Develop a relationship through giving. Hand out your knowledge, your expertise and guide them. You are able to do that by email and on the phone. Keep your prospect interested and updated with new information. Use Twitter, Facebook and You-tube videos and direct them onto your site. Befriend them!

Your Main Business

When you have formed a solid relationship

with your leads, you are able to direct them to your main business. Since it was often said before: 'People join people'.

They join you due to your individual personality: they trust you, they like you, since you bring value to them by providing them with the information they require.

There's always a possibility that a prospect won't join most of your business. Reasons can differ: they are, maybe, not ready yet; or maybe they have signed up to another company and wish to stick to it.

Regardless of any of this, you need to communicate with your prospects through emails so they will be able to join you over time. Should they not sign up to your main opportunity, you still could be profiting once they join your affiliate programs.

All of the first 4 steps above would be the front end of the funnel and your main income opportunity would be at the back-end. That's where the actual profit is!

So, in the event that you don't have a Sales Funnel in place yet, don't delay and obtain one NOW!

Content Marketing

With the advent of Google's Panda and Penguin update, the present rules about article promotion have changed and really should be labelled underneath the heading of content marketing.

Prior to the Google's 'Panda' Update, lots of article writers afforded only a passing thought to their content quality. Writing on the net became an exercise to find out who could out-think the various SE's (search engines) by publishing a minimal quantity of info and obtain the best traffic amounts.

The phrase: 'content marketing', has been associated more with the dissemination of information to clients and wasn't usually related to directly promoting an item.

The concept was that, to earn money writing, this content must give clients valuable information. Clients would then feel a sense of loyalty and continue to steadily buy from the vendor who was offering the good content in the shape of brochures, handouts, and web site content.

The philosophy is that, by educating the general public with, for example, educational material, the marketing company will be named a business expert and the brand would be much more likely to be purchased.

Content marketing isn't (any longer) limited by the corporate, big brand, name writers. The various SE's are making article writers produce informative, quality material.

What's quality content? If you ask 5 people that, you'll get 5 differing answers. Rather than getting opinions, let's observe how Google defines quality content.

Google's Official Weblog defines quality content websites as sites with unique content and information, such as: research, in-depth reports and thoughtful analysis.

But wait! That isn't all. They also say that grammar, relevancy and originality (or uniqueness) play essential parts in the pursuit of top quality content.

Relevancy in key words, relevancy of titles to

content, relevancy of content to your audience all plays a part.

Even though writing for the net is extremely forgiving (for the reason that anybody can publish just about any-thing), Google has adopted correct grammar as part of its' goal to greatly help folks have a much better search experience.

Finally, to create money writing, you have to think about the originality and uniqueness of the content. Articles must be well researched and supply helpful information.

On their official weblog, Google lists twenty-two questions that may provide you with guidance on the Google mind-set. The questions vary from: 'Would you be comfortable giving your charge card information for this site?', to: 'How much quality control is actioned on the content?'.

These questions, therefore, move from enquiring about trust to enquiring about grammar. The goal posts have, therefore, moved. Article writers wishing to become successful as marketers need to dedicate more focus to their content marketing.

Article Marketing

Working on the web is a really desirable career for people all over the world. Article promotion is a way that you are able to make (nearly) every business opportunity you participate in flourish into a self-sustained, profitable venture. In this chapter, we'll cover the best recommendations of the trade for implementing article promotion so you can get your name out there.

The impact of your articles can be boosted by telling stories or anecdotes together because readers love a narrative. Once they read your article, they'll pay more attention if they're engrossed in a story. Obviously, writing a great story is really a specialized skill. It requires more effort than several other types of content creation. The added popularity of narrative articles, though, may make it worth your time and effort.

By specializing your article to a select field or certain niche, you'll not only hone your articles to be most helpful but, additionally, you'll attract many more viewers from that field. Furthermore, there is less competition in the more specialised article marketing niches.

Your natural inclination might be to provide a fictionalized account of a service or product in your article promotion campaign. However, you must always remain truthful. If you're marketing something that you can't find any positive thing to express about, you definitely should be marketing another thing. Don't attempt to portray an item as wonderful if it's not, at the very least, good already.

Driving individuals to a particular site or product isn't the only means by which article promotion will pay off for you personally. A great deal of websites available (who will accept your write-ups) will, in actuality, pay you per view or per click. To help you find lots of methods to keep your earnings stream alive through the articles you write, this may become very lucrative.

For connecting better together with your readers within an article promotion program, focus your article on solving an issue for them. This can give your article a general purpose and theme, and it'll be one which readers' appreciate. Not just will a problem-solving article boost your rapport with readers, it'll gently nudge them towards buying your services or products.

Simply because working on-line is something you actually want to do, that does not mean that you'll be proficient at it. A terrific way to ensure your success would be to follow the advice given above whenever you make an effort to build your advertising campaign. Stay with the easy stuff to begin with, and you'll be able to branch out to bigger things.

Google's Adwords Program

Google AdWords is text-based system employed to promote various sites. This innovative service allows individuals to create their very own adverts, select key words to complement the intended audience's niche and determine the price of advertising. Advertisers take advantage of this great service simply because they pay only whenever a viewer clicks on the ad.

It has helped many businesses make their on-line presence felt using its unique features and is dependant on the actual Google search engine results. It provides results in line with the pages of a specific web site matched with the site's search and ad share. It's a great marketing tool making a big positive change to the amount and quality of visitors that review a webpage. Anyone who wishes to market their products and services can enrol with this service.

The AdWords program is preferable to all the conventional advertising programs since it targets people's particular interests. The creation and editing of adverts can be achieved within a few minutes and Adverts can quickly be observed by prospects straight after this. Advertisers may also get extensive performance reports to allow them to assess the potency of adverts by using this tool.

This kind of unique online marketing helps the advertisers to handle single and multiple adverts using one or many key words. This can help to create consistent website traffic for the advertiser's services and products. There's ample space for, at the very least, 8 to 10 advertisers on a solitary webpage. An advertiser can decide to book the topmost or maybe the most visible space on a webpage to create traffic for his or her site.

Google AdWords may also help an advertiser to find out the profitability, quantity and type of searches that individuals or potential customers do. This is often helpful for SEO purposes too. The advertisers may use the tool to create changes within their sites to obtain top rankings in major search results.

This internet marketing tool is ideal for those who have just started their business and don't have big bucks to market their products and services. Regardless of how small the budget of a company is, it may still make use of this service. There is absolutely no minimum monthly charge. Google only charges a little activation fee for the advertisement. Advertisers also have the choice of choosing among text, image, and video adverts.

Google AdWords has changed the way in which people advertise their services and products. It will not only retain old clients but, additionally, attract new clients to a company as well. Consequently, your brand name becomes popular and your sales will increase.

Marketing Offline

The primary aim for any business would be to turn prospective buyers in to actual buyers. Many marketers have questioned the potency of offline marketing to enhance on-line sales, however, they are related if the campaign is performed precisely and has enough substance to stimulate the web marketing opportunity.

You will find so many products and services that it's difficult to state for definite that offline marketing can greatly boost your online marketing efforts. The rewards for creating an enticing direct mail campaign might help your web conversions but this, in conjunction with using the right list and the best offer, remains the key to the success of the web income opportunity.

Here are some key offline creative techniques to produce an engaging direct mail campaign which will directly affect your web conversions:

The Package. You have to plan the direct mail package and the primary focus should be on exactly what it will include. Most marketers begin with a letter, an action call and a return envelope. You could play around with this approach but the fundamentals will always be the same. Work-out how large it will likely be and what creative course of action to take. Much of this is determined by your industry as well as your audience.

The Envelope. If the prospective audience recognises your envelope as spam, they're not going to even open it and your offer is useless if no-body sees it. Provide the customer an incentive to open your envelope and find out more about your product, service and deal. Do some research on other direct mail campaigns that compelled you to open the envelope and view the offer.

Value Postcards. If your company has a budget restriction for this kind of marketing, then the utilization of postcards could be a good way of keeping your costs low. The inclusion of postcards can steer clear of the problem of unopened mail and they may be an effective way of driving individuals to an on-line offer. This is so long as the offer is gripping enough to motivate them to go to the web site. Be sure you have a distinctive URL for the visitors included on them.

An Action Call. This should be clear and readily accessible by the client. A great way is to produce a multi-order system, telephone call, on-line or fax order form. The action call should be bold and no nonsense. Make certain the ordering process is straightforward as this can encourage the client to return for multiple purchases.

Begin with an easy campaign and an offer that's simple to track and manage. Test an inexpensive direct mail campaign in the beginning and you might discover that this drives traffic and sales to your online business.

Blogs

With regards to business, blogs can be a supplemental type of advertising that can be used to communicate with your clients. On top of that, blogs can be set-up free of charge and may easily stand alone, with no existing site to help them.

Blogs have ended up being quite well-liked and a growing number of blogs are appearing on multiple web sites. Blogs serve as business tools and people adore communicating with others via blog postings and allowing others to discuss their comments.

Blogs are regularly updated so they have fresh

content on them constantly. This makes them attractive to visitors and SE's like Google. Each new post counts as unique content on the site and, should you add to your blog weekly or daily, you will notice it expanding rather rapidly. With new content, you are able to rank higher in the search engine results positioning and draw more people to your site.

Additionally, you can include links on your blogs and begin a hyper-link exchange campaign. In doing this, you will see your page ranking upsurge in the SE's due to the fact that SE algorithms usually focus on the amount of links which are pointing to your site. The greater the number of external links that point to your site, the simpler it will be to be discovered by the big SE's.

Blogs might be employed to freely advertise your goods or services. Also, blogs are excellent for providing existing clients with updated details about new services and products you might be offering. Want your customers to talk about their feelings about your services and products? You'll be able to use blogs to get and share client testimonials. There certainly isn't any limit to the advantages you are able to experience with blogs.

What's equally great about blogs is the truth that you are able to produce them free of charge. Sites like Blogger (purchased by Google), let you begin a weblog totally free. More-over, there are numerous fonts, templates and layouts to choose from and Blogger will even enable you to display pictures. Finally, web sites like Blogger provide you with the opportunity to archive your postings to ensure visitors can go back to them over and over.

Making blogs is enjoyable and easy for everyone. Blogging is the new wave in Internet advertising that allows you to get up close, personal and interactive with your prospects on a daily basis. Communicate with individuals from across the world who share the very passions that your business caters to. Find out what they want and what they think about what you currently provide.

Before the internet, no other form of advertising even came close to offering this scope for customer engagement.

Social Media

In the event that you have not started using social media marketing, you might want to have a closer look. Not just are you missing a strong marketing tool, you are potentially missing being seen by potential customers who're being driven to your competitors who're using this marketing medium.

It's no secret that many people head to the net to find information nowadays. Including to find the services and products they require. Instead of searching via a printed phone book, it's much more likely that they're going to visit a common internet search engine.

Due to this, S.E.O. (search engine optimization) has been, probably, one of the most highly promoted marketing tools recently. These kinds of searches, however, await a prospective customer to become active. Promoting companies through social networking can generate a nearly passive response following the first initial click.

Facebook, for instance, probably one of the most commonly visited websites every day on line, enables you to produce a fan-page for your company. Somebody 'Likes' your company by clicking a button and becomes a fan.

Once somebody becomes your fan, a notice is posted for their own profile page so their friends can easily see this and may then choose to go and see what your fan-page is about. At that time, a number of them could decide to become fans of your business.

Additionally, each time you post something to your company fan-page, these details can also be delivered to the news feed for your fans and is then visible to many of their friends.

Everybody knows that person-to-person advertising may be the most effective form of advertising that exists. A Facebook fan-page is a combination of person-to-person advertising and viral marketing.

Simply by creating that page, you'll be able to reach people that you might not have found when you are introduced to them by your fans. When potential individuals are introduced to you in this manner, they're more likely to wish to support your company.

Other social networking outlets, such as Twitter and LinkedIn, work in a very similar way. Among the best facets of this whole genre is that it's a totally free, or really low cost, approach to potentially reach huge numbers of people.

With a tiny bit of daily effort, you are able to keep your organization at the forefront of the minds of everybody who's part of the social network.

Social media marketing isn't something you ought to be considering for future years. It's here, at this time and you ought to be utilizing it.

Because the primary investment to get started is simply a tiny bit of time, it certainly is sensible to begin as quickly as possible.

Auto Responders

An auto-responder service is really a 'must have' service included in an Internet marketer's box of tools. Together with your subscription for this on-line service, the marketer can put up a contact message to automatically be sent to his / her list each week to stay in touch with their subscribers. Here are a few tactics we've discovered that work well:

When employing your auto-responder to recommend the purchase of a service or product, you need to be careful the way you word your messages. Keep building on what your prospect's problem is and how your service or product can solve that problem for them.

In your first email, welcome them and thank them for subscribing to your list. Let them know the benefits they'll receive from you, such as: free ebooks, free audio recordings and free computer software. You're getting them to truly like you and build trust. Don't sell them anything in the very first email message.

In the 2nd email to your list, send them 2-3 links where they are able to visit sites to obtain free related products to your niche but, this time around, make your second and third links 'affiliate links' from other marketers' websites you have joined as an affiliate.

They are still free products and services, such as: free membership to a website that provides many free items. You hide your longer affiliate link using tinyurl.com so you don't tip them off. When they click on it (as they have become accustomed to do) they will go to the free membership site (or whatever item it is), get the free item and (hopefully) also buy one of the other items for sale.

In the 3rd email for them, send them 3 links where they are able to obtain a free software package, a totally free audio, or perhaps a free ebook. Again, you need to send them the 2nd and third link as a disguised affiliate link that you could earn a commission on. This is the way you build your sales with auto-responder emails.

With each email message, make sure you are giving the client free information associated with the subject. It's this that could keep them interested.

It is probable that, by the fourth email to your list, many people may have bought a few of the products and services available (i.e. those that are also offered by the free websites) and that you begin to see some commission payments enter your pay-pal account.

Remember, it's a popular fact in marketing that visitors frequently need to be subjected to an offer seven times before they decide to purchase. Sales may begin slowly, but just getting it started is the biggest challenge.

The Joint Venture

In the event that you sign up for newsletters and mailing lists from marketing specialists, you might have run into the word 'JV' or 'Joint Venture'. Essentially, a JV is a partnership of sorts, although not in the legal sense.

A JV may take many forms, but it's mostly about collaboration - working together to produce better results than each one of you can achieve by yourself.

Listed here are just some ways you can 'JV'

with others:

Tele-seminars and workshops - Partner with a person who is serving an identical kind of client to you to provide workshops where the delegates will get several perspectives (and also you share the job involved with organising and marketing the big event).

Creating Products and services - By yourself, developing a product (like a CD or on-line course) may appear daunting but, in the event that you use another person, you are able to brainstorm some ideas and take action in a fraction of the time. Plus, you are able to each market the merchandise to your personal databases of clients and customers.

Product Launches/Special Offers - We recently teamed up with some others who help coaches to promote themselves to advertise a book of ours relating to this topic. They donated a totally free bonus and marketed the book for their e-mail lists - everyone profited. People purchasing the book got an excellent group of bonuses and heard about sites where they could find extra information on marketing. The folks providing the bonuses got additional exposure and PR.

Joint Bidding/Pitching - You might face tough competition when you are bidding or pitching for corporate or government contracts but, with a little team of associates, you are able to stand a far greater chance in the event that you pool your expertise, testimonials and resources.

Affiliates - You are able to either be a joint venture partner for another person's products and services and promote them as a swap for a commission, or look for affiliates to advertise your personal products and services, paying them a commission once the sales are made.

One good free site to get involved with is jvme.com, which is a leading joint venture social network run by internet marketers via Facebook's base software applications.

Whenever you're thinking about doing a JV, one thing to be clear about up-front is how much money and time each of you will be investing and how you will distribute the profits when they come in.

The best option here is to be transparent at the start and keep costs to the minimum required to do the job well.

JVs, with the right people and the right companies, can work wonders for you and they don't have to be as daunting or on such a large scale as some people would have you believe.

Measuring Success

There are several different tools on the market that can help you gauge the success of your sales funnel efforts. In this chapter, we will provide a brief overview of a few of the more popular ones:

Google Analytics is a terrific way to examine how well your web store is working. Once you have built-in Analytics together with your store pages, you are able to access an enormous selection of helpful reports.

Google Analytics enables you to set-up a sales funnel and see just how many individuals are deferring at every step of your funnel. That ought to alert you to which areas of the funnel process you need to improve.

Say that, for each 1,000 people who visit your product page:

100 add the merchandise for their cart
80 of these people go to the checkout
40 of these people complete the checkout form
33 of these people confirm their order

Out of this example, it's clear that many shoppers (fifty percent) are leaving the purchasing procedure when they are asked to fill out the check-out form. This could imply that there's something about the form that's off-putting to people.

StatCounter is also a web tracking service that enables you to access up-to-date statistics about web visitors throughout several sites.

Just like a standard web-stat tool, you'll have the ability to see the details of your unique site visitors, visitors that return, page loadings, and 1st time site visitors. You can observe the information presented daily, weekly, monthly, quarterly, annually as well as choose specific date ranges.

Over-all, Statcounter is a good tool while offering all you need to help make the necessary changes to your website.

Smartsheet.com is a spreadsheet with special features that allows you (among other things) to track company objectives and operations and manage projects and deliverables by teams and individuals. This is a comprehensive solution for strategy analysis.

The sales funnel estimator at mathmarketing.com allows you to approximate your market profitability and calculate precisely what quantity of purchases you can expect from a sales funnel and what quantity of prospects you require at the top of your funnel to reach your targets.

ClickBank Analytics provides you with the capability to interactively set-up trend charts based on different topics over customized time ranges. Data and chart tables are supplied to help you witness sales trends along with the information that supports everything in a single glance. Also, the charts could be manipulated in various ways, letting you begin to see the trends you'll need to handle your company.

It's well worth taking the time to acquire and familiarise yourself with these tools because they can highlight vital areas for improvement in your campaigns that you would be unable to identify in any other way.

Top Sales Funnel Products

As well as being a good source of affiliate products for you to promote, Clickbank also sells a number of ebooks and software relating to sales funnels which you would be advised to acquire when you are first starting out. Below, we will give a brief description of a few of the better ebooks (and other items) about this subject that Clickbank features:

'The Silent Sales Machine' by Jim Cockrum is one of the best selling ebooks on Clickbank. It has been sold since 2002 and details a myriad of techniques for creating a recurring income online with a minimum of start up capital and little or no ongoing maintenance required. It has been updated for 2011 and focuses on E-bay auctions and the power-selling of particular products.

'The Profit Pulling Sales Funnel' by Ben Brooks, shows you how to attract targeted buyer traffic to your website free of charge from a little known traffic source using article marketing.

The 'TAP Profit Funnel' by Grant J Ferrari, is an unorthodox affiliate marketing system for beginners using Twitter that only take 15 minutes per day to operate. It shows you how to build a sales focused audience on Twitter quickly then sell Clickbank products to them.

The 'Video Sales Letter Creator' is some innovative software that will let you professionally video market your products with very little user input. If you use Wordpress, it also comes with a Wordpress plug in so it will work with your theme. It comes with a whole raft of features for customization and there are no monthly fees to pay.

'Sales, Lies & Naked Truths' by Corrine Edwards is a book aimed at all salespeople wanting the most up-to-date, modern sales techniques. The methods in this book do away with the out-dated 'hard sell' methods and are aimed more at making you genuine and likeable in the eyes of the customer. This ensures that they will purchase from YOU after you've established an honest relationship with them.

Finally, 'Sales CSI' by Rick Braddy is a complete course on how to maximize the returns from your current marketing campaigns including list building, Google Adwords, Facebook advertising and how to cut out any wasted spending on advertising that you might be unknowingly making at the moment. This is a unique video training program that outlines where you should concentrate your SEO efforts to increase your ROI substantially.

These ebooks, courses and software can all be a useful source of information for budding online entrepreneurs and even for more for experienced people who want to expand their knowledge or capabilities into different areas.

You are advised to do your own research, as well, because the full quantity of resources available on the internet relating to this subject is, obviously, far too big to completely do justice to here.

CPSIA information can be obtained
at www.ICGtesting.com
Printed in the USA
BVHW090120230421
605635BV00001B/75

 9 781802 664515